HURRICANE
DESTRUCTION

by

Dougal Dixon

WATERBIRD BOOKS

Columbus, Ohio

EXPEDITION EARTH

HURRICANE DESTRUCTION

by Dougal Dixon

Mc Graw Hill **Children's Publishing**

© ticktock Entertainment Ltd. 2004

First published in Great Britain in 2004 by ticktock Media Ltd.,

Unit 2, Orchard Business Centre, North Farm Road, Tunbridge Wells, Kent, TN2 3XF

We would like to thank David Gillingwater and Elizabeth Wiggans

Illustrations by John Alston and David Gillingwater

This edition published in the United States of America in 2004 by

Waterbird Books, an imprint of

McGraw-Hill Children's Publishing,

a Division of the McGraw-Hill Companies

8787 Orion Place

Columbus, Ohio 43240-4027

www.MHkids.com

Library of Congress Cataloging-in-Publication Data is on file with the publisher.

t=top, b=bottom, c=center, l=left, r=right, OFC=outside front cover, OBC=outside back cover

Alamy: 14-15 main, 16t, 17t, 24-25c. Index Stock: OFC. NOAA: 6t & 6b, 7t & 7c, 8-9 all, 10-11 all, 12-13 all, 15b, 22b, 26b, 27t all. Red Cross: 24b.

Every effort has been made to trace the copyright holders, and we apologize in advance for any unintentional omissions. We would be pleased to insert the appropriate acknowledgements in any subsequent edition of this publication.

Printed in China

1-57768-868-6

1 2 3 4 5 6 7 8 9 10 TTM 09 08 07 06 05 04

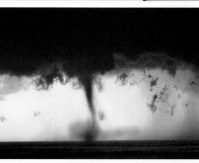

CONTENTS

DAY 1
Location: The Hurricane *news station*

Hi. My name is Robbie James, and I'm fascinated by hurricanes. This summer, I am an intern for an area newspaper called *The Hurricane*. To learn more about wind and storms, I interviewed a scientist who studies wind conditions. While I was asking him about his work, his telephone rang. The scientist runs a team of hurricane experts who fly all over the world studying this phenomenon. It is hurricane season now in the Atlantic Ocean. The team is about to set off in pursuit of a hurricane, but one of the crew can't make it. There is a spare seat on the plane, and the scientist invited me on board to see how hurricanes work. It will be exciting but dangerous.

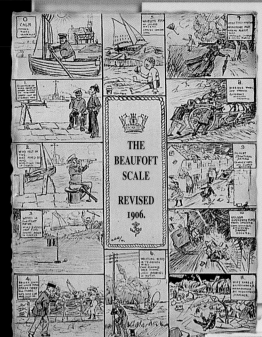

BEAUFORT SCALE
We measure wind speed on a scale called the Beaufort scale. This scale was first devised by Admiral Francis Beaufort in 1806. It ranges from 0 (calm) to 12 (hurricane).

GREAT WAVES
Coastal nations have always been aware of the danger of storms and hurricanes. This Japanese art features mountainous waves caused by huge winds. Japanese islands have long been affected by hurricanes.

This is a poster of my favorite film, *Twister*. It is about tornadoes that cause chaos across America.

TWISTER

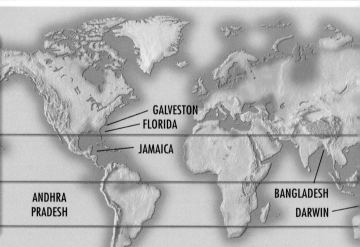

GALVESTON
FLORIDA
JAMAICA
ANDHRA PRADESH
BANGLADESH
DARWIN

Hurricanes begin at sea between the Tropics of Cancer and Capricorn. As the earth turns, hurricanes move westward. They often curve away from the equator and hit islands and eastern coastlines. This maps shows the world's hurricane hotspots.

HOW WIND IS FORMED

Wind is caused by warm air rising and cool air rushing in to take its place. In places where there is a big difference between the temperature of the warm air and that of the cool air, winds become very strong.

INSIDE A HURRICANE

Hurricanes begin as tropical storms over the warm waters of the Atlantic and Pacific Oceans near the equator. As the ocean water evaporates, it rises until a huge column of warm, moist air is twisted high into the atmosphere. The low pressure at the center, called the *eye*, causes the ocean surface to bulge upward. As the system moves westward, it pushes a dangerous surge of ocean water ahead of it.

From space, a hurricane looks like a wispy spiral. Its beauty hides the howling chaos beneath.

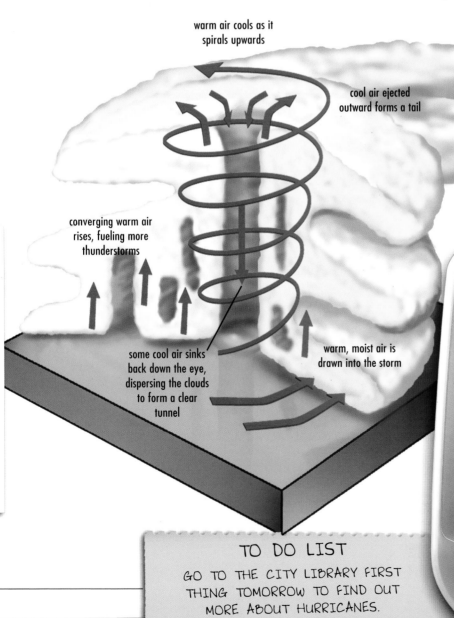

warm air cools as it spirals upwards

cool air ejected outward forms a tail

converging warm air rises, fueling more thunderstorms

some cool air sinks back down the eye, dispersing the clouds to form a clear tunnel

warm, moist air is drawn into the storm

Tropic of Cancer

Equator

Tropic of Capricorn

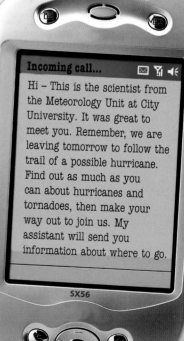

Incoming call...

Hi – This is the scientist from the Meteorology Unit at City University. It was great to meet you. Remember, we are leaving tomorrow to follow the trail of a possible hurricane. Find out as much as you can about hurricanes and tornadoes, then make your way out to join us. My assistant will send you information about where to go.

SX56

TO DO LIST
GO TO THE CITY LIBRARY FIRST THING TOMORROW TO FIND OUT MORE ABOUT HURRICANES.

DAY 2
Location: *The City Library*

Great! I am so excited about going on the hurricane hunters' plane. First, though, I have to find out all I can about hurricanes.

I am at City Library looking at reports of old hurricane disasters. There was a big hurricane in Galveston, Texas at the beginning of the 20th century. This was the strongest hurricane that ever struck the continental United States. Before that time, Galveston was the most important port on the Gulf coast of Texas, controling America's valuable cotton trade. It was also developing as a holiday resort and was becoming one of the most prosperous cities in the United States. All of that was destroyed in the year 1900 when floods and high wind pounded the area for two days. The hurricane traveled in from the Atlantic Ocean, swept across the Caribbean Islands and across the Gulf of Mexico before it smashed into Galveston.

Taken from
The Hurricane, September 9, 1900

FLOODS HIT TOWN OF GALVESTON

For days, the hurricane had been increasing in strength, causing damage to the Caribbean Islands 600 miles to the east. It looked as though the hurricane would not reach the Gulf coast and mainland America. But, by dawn yesertday, waves began to pound the beach and the natural habitat of Galveston. A surge of water, driven by the approaching hurricane, swamped the town (most of which was above sea level). The water cut off the passageway to the mainland. By midday, the main forces of the hurricane had reached land. Today, the people of Galveston, Texas are trying to determine how much damage the floods and high winds caused during the hurricane.

The paper I write for has been in existance for over 100 years!

SACRED HEART CHURCH CRUMBLES

At least 400 people took refuge in Galveston's Sacred Heart Church as the winds began to build. The building was the city's only stone-made structure built on proper foundations. The hurricane was too strong for the church, though. After the hurricane had passed, only two steeples and a broken shell remained. There was no sign of the hundreds of people who had sought sanctuary there. All around lay the ruins of the wooden buildings that destroyed most of the city. Their sandy foundations had been swept away by the floods. The timber structures disintegrated, and any leftover fragments were carried off.

CITY LIBRARY

Robbie James
STUDENT

24515521 522

Taken from
The Hurricane, September 10, 1900

UNITED STATES

Galveston

Caribbean islands

Taken from *The Hurricane,* June 10, 1900

DEATH TOLL HITS 6,000

The death toll of this week's hurricane in Galveston is likely to reach 6,000, or about 15 percent of the population. The victims are being buried at sea to avoid contagious diseases. It is estimated that 2,600 homes have been destroyed, and 10,000 people are now homeless.

Taken from *The Hurricane,* June 10, 1990

TOWN MAKES PLANS FOR FUTURE SAFETY

After the hurricane of 1900, Galveston was rebuilt with a defensive sea wall. Most of the damage that was caused in 1900 was due to the fact that the city is so close to sea level, making it vulnerable to storm surges. The defensive measures proved to be successful. Another hurricane in 1915 caused only a dozen casualties, and others in 1961 and 1983 resulted in relatively minor damage. The city has never achieved the importance that it had before 1900, though.

Taken from *The Hurricane,* March 1, 1901

GALVESTON'S INDUSTRY DESTROYED

The farmland behind Galveston has lost its cotton crop to the hurricane. This is not only a problem for the area residents, it is also likely to cause severe problems in the textile industries of Europe, which depend on Galveston's cotton.

DAY 3
Location: The *City Library*

Although hurricanes, like the one that hit Galveston, have taught us a great deal about storms and damage prevention, each new hurricane still catches people by surprise. On August 24, 1992, a massive hurricane struck southern Florida. It was named *Hurricane Andrew*, and it became one of the most powerful hurricanes to hit the mainland of the United States in recorded history. Just like in Galveston, the first damage was done by gigantic waves that pushed ahead of the hurricane itself. The center of the hurricane moved across the state at a speed of 20 miles per hour, but the winds around the center spun up to 200 miles per hour. The wind pulled boats out of the coastal area, turned over vehicles, destroyed mobile homes, and wrecked everything in its path. Even though the hurricane arrived on land two days before the meteorologists predicted, over one million people were able to evacuate their homes in time. Those who did not leave took refuge in public hurricane shelters or house basements, and there was surprisingly little loss of life.

FLORIDA UNPREPARE[D] FOR MONSTER WIND[S]

The people of Florida were not concerned ab[out] hurricanes. There had been no serious hurricanes to [hit] land since the 1950s, and for four decades the suburbs [of] Miami expanded and developed with little regard to [a] disaster that could strike.

Even when Hurricane Andrew began to form out in [the] Atlantic, there was no sense of urgency. Initial rep[orts] suggested that the hurricane would travel up the east[ern] seaboard. But, it changed direction, leaving the people [of] Florida with little time to prepare.

MILLIONS OF DOLLARS OF DAMAGE CAUSED BY HURRICANE ANDREW

Hurricane Andrew was one of the most expensive hurricanes on record. More than 80,000 homes were destroyed, and another 55,000 were badly damaged in Florida alone. The hurricane flattened an area the size of Chicago. It continued on, hitting New Orleans where it caused more damage. In the end, Hurricane Andrew caused about 25 billion dollars worth of damage in Florida. Amazingly, there were only 50 fatalities.

Taken from
The Hurricane, August 31, 1992

DESPERATE SURVIVORS

Upon returning to their Florida homes, survivors found no infrastructure left. Electricity and piped water were gone. An influx of 16,000 troops helped to maintain order while relief workers from all over the country began to restore normality to the region.

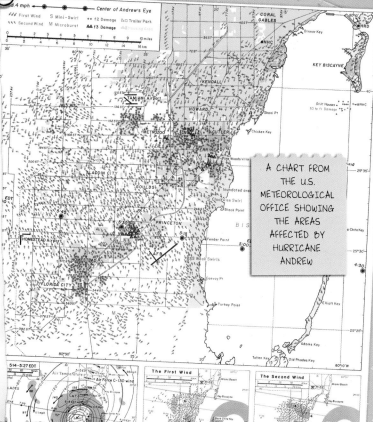

A CHART FROM THE U.S. METEOROLOGICAL OFFICE SHOWING THE AREAS AFFECTED BY HURRICANE ANDREW

Before Hurricane Andrew, Florida was regarded as one of the best places in the United States to live. The destruction caused by the hurricane showed just how vulnerable the state was to natural disasters. About 25,000 people left the area and never returned.

Now that I have done all of this research, I'm not sure if I want to see a hurricane up close!

Incoming call...

Hi Robbie—This is the scientist's assistant. Can you make it to City Airport by 10 A.M. tomorrow morning? We would like to leave on time. We think that there are storms brewing out in the Atlantic, and we don't want to miss the action.

SX56

DAY 4 (Morning)

Location: *The City airport*

What a thrill! I have never been on an airplane like this one before. When you fly somewhere on vacation, you have a comfortable seat, a movie to watch, and a flight attendant to bring you drinks. Things are very different here. This is a working plane. Everybody here has a job to do. There is not much room for all of us. The equipment, which looks like a mass of dials and computer screens, takes up most of the space.

The scientist is the leader of the team. He says there is a hurricane beginning to form just out over the ocean, and we are going to take a look at it. He says that we are going to fly right into the center of the storm. I don't like the sound of that, but the pilot thinks it will be okay.

The scientist gave me this funny little sketch showing what everybody does on the plane.

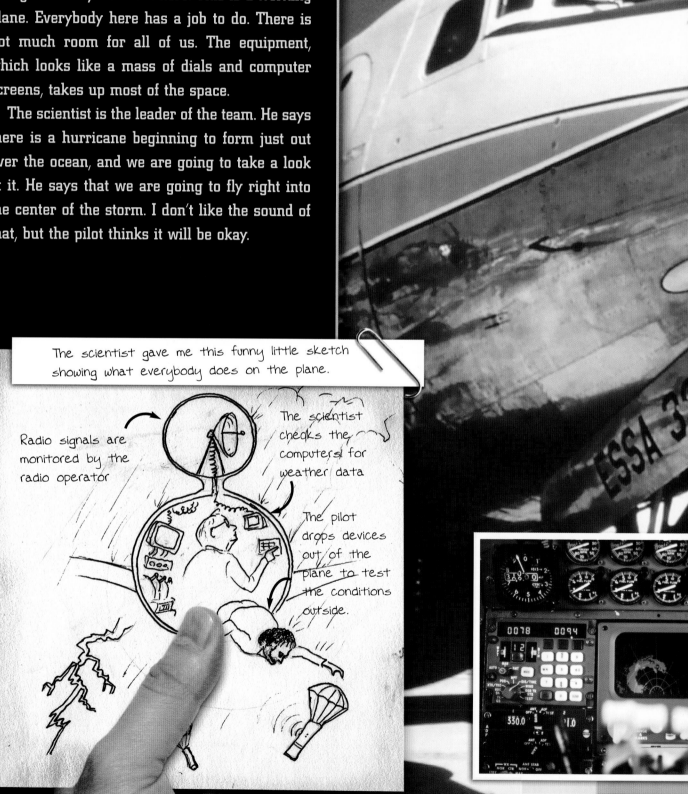

Radio signals are monitored by the radio operator

The scientist checks the computers for weather data

The pilot drops devices out of the plane to test the conditions outside.

WATCH YOUR WINGS!
Big, heavy, specialized airplanes like ours are not only sent out to monitor hurricanes. When numerous thunderstorms develop at sea, aircraft like ours are sometimes sent out to see how the storms are developing.

The Scientist is the senior meteorologist. He has been studying hurricanes for a very long time.

The Pilot is the person who controls the plane. He flies many air-sea rescue missions, so he is familiar with bad weather.

The Co-Pilot provides support to the pilot during the storm. He monitors all of the plane's system lights.

The Engineer cares for the storm-tracking equipment. He fixes things when they go wrong.

The Radio Operator takes signals from the ground to help the pilot plot the course safely.

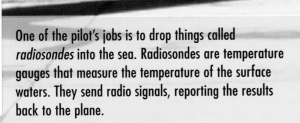

One of the pilot's jobs is to drop things called *radiosondes* into the sea. Radiosondes are temperature gauges that measure the temperature of the surface waters. They send radio signals, reporting the results back to the plane.

DAY 4 (Afternoon)

Location: *The hurricane has started to develop out in the Atlantic Ocean.*

After several hours of flying in clear weather, we began to see wisps of clouds high above us. At the same time, our view of the ocean below us became obscured—first by separate fluffy clouds, and then by continuous cloud cover. Then, we flew into the clouds themselves. For the past hour or so, it has been getting darker and darker as we have flown deeper into the hurricane itself.

The airplane is creaking and shaking. The crew does not seem to notice. They are all very busy studying their instruments.

Suddenly, we are in bright sunlight again. I thought that we were out of the hurricane, but the scientist tells me that we have entered the quiet spot at the center around which everything rotates. This is called the *eye*. As soon as we reenter the clouds, the turbulence will start again.

ROUTE

We are not alone here. A high-altitude jet is taking readings above the hurricane. When we compare our findings, we will be able to find out more about how a hurricane works.

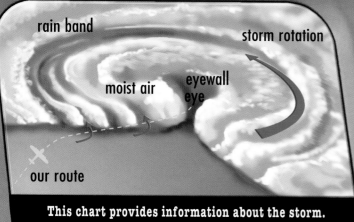

rain band

storm rotation

moist air

eyewall
eye

our route

This chart provides information about the storm. We are heading right into the eye where we should be safe.

HURRICANE NAMES

After World War II, it was decided to give names to hurricanes to distinguish one from another. Originally, only female names were used but then in 1970, it was considered to be politically incorrect to use only female names. Now, every year, meteorologists compile an alphabetic list of alternating male and female names. When a hurricane develops, the meteorologists assign it the next name on the list.

We are picking up an image of the hurricane. The different colors indicate the varying temperatures. The cool air near the eye appears up as gray and blue and the warmer air as yellow and red.

AUSTRALIAN METEOROLOGIST CLEMENT WRAGGE (1852-1922) was the first to give names to hurricanes. He used the names of people he did not like!

DAY 4 (Evening)

Location: *Somewhere in the Caribbean*

I knew we should never have flown into a hurricane! We were just asking for trouble.

In one spot of bad turbulence there was a terrible grinding noise from the back of the plane. The engineer said something about the tail falling off. I took it as a joke but then noticed that everybody else looked nervous. The radio operator sent out a distress message, and the pilot immediately turned the plane away from the hurricane to look for a safe place to land. Everybody stopped work and strapped down the equipment.

Luckily, we were not far away from a group of tiny Caribbean islands. We had to stop on the islands for repairs. Now, we will not have time to perform all the studies we were hoping to complete. I am just glad that we landed safely.

The island chain is a string of small volcanic islands at the edge of the Caribbean. Because of their location, the islands have been victim to hurricanes throughout their history.

AIRPORT

Our emergency landing brought us to an island that was in the middle of celebrating a religious festival!

This is a hurricane probability map. The red area shows where the hurricane will definitely strike. The islands are in the yellow area, where the hurricane may or may not strike. We may just be safe.

TECHNICIAN'S REPORT

- Repairs urgently need to be made to the plane.
- Rudder was severely twisted and battered by the winds.
- Further flight in this condition is impossible.
- Estimated time for repairs: seven days.

It looks like we will be here for another week!

DAY 5
Location: *The Caribbean*

It looks as though we have landed in the wrong place. Reports coming in from the meteorological stations show that the hurricane has moved to the southwest, and the islands we are on are right in its path. Hurricanes are unpredictable. The strange thing is that everything here seems so normal. It is a bright, sunny day with only a few wisps of very high clouds. There is a camera crew on the island filming the local carnival, and they are carrying on with their work.

However, the local people do seem to be concerned. They are cutting back vegetation from around their houses and pegging down the lighter buildings. The police have issued a hurricane watch and are handing out cards that remind the islanders how to prepare for a possible hurricane.

Later

The authorities have now upgraded the hurricane watch to a hurricane warning. This urges people to make serious preparations.

LOCALS FEEL THE POWER OF CYCLONE TRACY—MERRY CHRISTMAS, DARWIN!

A cyclone, which is the Australian word for *hurricane*, has caught Northern Territories of Australia by surprise. Cyclone Tracy was predicted to head southwestward across the Timor Sea. Without warning, on Christmas Eve, it suddenly swung ninety degrees to the southeast and struck the city of Darwin on the northern coast. The sheer surprise caught the citizens unprepared, and half of them were left homeless.

Cut out from
The Hurricane, December 25, 1974

Special road signs have been set up to guide people to safety in the event of a hurricane.

HURRICANE DOS AND DON'TS
Safety Actions
BEFORE HURRICANE SEASON

- Find out if your home meets current building code requirements for high winds. Experts agree that structures built to meet or exceed current building code high-wind provisions have a much better chance of surviving violent windstorms. For more info visit www.ibhs.org
- Protect all windows by installing commercial shutters or plywood panels.
- Garage doors are frequently the first feature in a home to fail, so reinforce all garage doors so that they can withstand high winds.
- If you do not live in an evacuation zone or a mobile home, designate an interior room with no windows or external doors as a "Safe Room."
- If you do live in an evacuation zone or a mobile home, be prepared to leave your home and temporarily relocate to somewhere else until the threat of the hurricane is over.
- Before hurricane season, assess your property to ensure that landscaping and trees do not become wind hazards.
- Trim dead wood and weak, overhanging branches from all trees.
- Certain trees and bushes are vulnerable to high winds. Any dead tree near a home is a hazard.

Here is a leaflet the scientist picked up from the U.S. Meteorological office.

EVACUATION ROUTE

The local people are preparing for the hurricane. They have been through this before.

The film crew is ignoring the warnings. They want to get out where the action is taking place. I hope they will be safe.

This leaflet is being been handed out to villagers to tell them what to do if the hurricane strikes.

High Wind Safety Actions AS A HURRICANE APPROACHES

- No mobile home is safe in hurricane force winds. Those residents should evacuate to a safer structure once local officials issue a hurricane evacuation order for their community.
- Once a hurricane warning is issued, install your window shutters or plywood panels.
- When a hurricane warning is issued for your community, secure or bring inside all lawn furniture and other outside objects that could become missiles in high winds.
- Listen carefully for safety instructions from local officials, and go to your designated "safe room" when directed to do so.
- Monitor N.O.A.A. (National Oceanic and Atmospheric Administration) Weather Radio.
- Do not leave your "safe room" until directed to do so by local officials, even if it appears that the winds have calmed down. Remember that there is little or no wind in the eye of a hurricane.

DAY 6
Location: *The north of the island*

Now we can really tell that a hurricane is coming. The low pressure in the hurricane's eye makes the sea level rise, and the movement of the system pushes the high water along. During the night, the sea rose up, and huge waves battered the causeways and bridges that connect the smaller islands to the main island. The authorities are trying to get everybody onto the main island, but the damage and the increasing winds are making the evacuation very difficult.

The film crew is on hand to take pictures, but they have already lost a lot of their equipment. One of their cars was washed away with their cameras and film inside.

The radio operator is still in our broken plane. He is monitoring the satellite transmissions and the information from other weather stations. It looks as if the hurricane is getting close.

Despite working together to combat the rising sea level, the local people will need to be evacuated.

BANGLADESH FLOODED AGAIN

Because it is so low-lying, Bangladesh is no stranger to flooding. Today, though, it has suffered an unparalleled catastrophe. A 20-foot high storm surge that formed ahead of Cyclone Gorky has submerged the low-lying islands and the sand spits. Thousands of homes have been flooded. The winds of the cyclone itself are now hammering the survivors of this initial surge.

Clipping from
The Hurricane, April 29, 1991

People are trying to go on with their daily routines despite rising waters.

Cars stand in deep water as the sea level continues to rise. People's homes are going to be under threat if this continues. There is nothing we can do but wait.

PATH OF THE **HURRICANE**

Wednesday 10:00 A.M.

Two days ago, the course of the hurricane was unpredictable. It looked as if it would pass to the north of the islands.

Thursday 4:00 P.M.

Satellite images show increasing wind speeds (red represents the strongest wind speed). The storm has changed course and is moving in the drirection of the islands.

Friday 9:00 A.M.

Today, the hurricane is almost upon us, and it is strengthening. The eye has become very small (a sign of increasing intensity), and the winds are stronger.

19

DAY 6 (Afternoon)
Location: *The island's capital*

We have taken shelter in the town hall's basement along with many of the locals. There are enough supplies in here to keep us going for days. Above us, we can hear a continuous roaring and rumbling as the hurricane wreaks havoc. Despite the fact that the basement is deep underground, the walls are vibrating.

I feel sorry for the poor film crew. They are still outside somewhere. At least they will be getting some spectacular footage. I hope that they are safe.

The scientist is with me. He first said that he thought the hurricane would be quite small, about a 2 on the Saffir-Simpson scale. This is a scale on which the strength of the hurricane is measured. The scientist now thinks the storm is intensifying to a level 3 or 4. The island is definitely taking a pounding above us.

9:00 A.M. *Wind and waves are starting to pick up.*

11:00 A.M. *A tornando! These sometimes occur close to the center of hurricanes but are not often caught on film.*

1:00 P.M. *Winds are now gusting to over 120 mph.*

5:00 P.M. *Suddenly, it is calm. Is the danger over?*

9:00 A.M.

11:00 A.M.

DEFINITION OF THE SAFFIR/SIMPSON SCALE

CATEGORY	WINDS (mph)	SURGE (ft)	EXAMPLES: FLORIDA COAST
1	74-95	4-5	AGNES 1972
2	96-110	6-8	CLEO 1964
3	111-130	9-12	BETSY 1965
4	131-155	13-18	DONNA 1960
5	GREATER THAN 155	GREATER THAN 18	1935 STORM

The Saffir-Simpson Scale measures a hurricane's strength based on the speed of the winds and the height of the storm surge.

FUJITA SCALE

	Wind Speed	Damage
F0	40-73 mph	Light
F1	74-112 mph	Moderate
F2	113-157 mph	Considerable
F3	158-206 mph	Severe
F4	207-260 mph	Devastating
F5	261-318 mph	Incredible

The Fujita Scale measures the strength of tornadoes, which are whirling columns of wind that often accompany hurricanes.

A nearby meteorological station made this radar image of the hurricane. It is right over the islands.

:00 p.m.

5:00 p.m.

Incoming...

Hello. Is anybody there? It's the co-pilot here. I am near the harbor with the film crew. Everything seems to have stopped. Is the hurricane over? Why don't you come out and take a look. We'll be waiting for you.

SX56

DAY 6 (Late Afternoon)
Location: *The island harbor*

The co-pilot was right. It is calm outside. The town is in ruins and is dripping wet, but the sun is shining, and there is no wind. None of the local people have come up to join us, though. They must know something that we don't.

The scientist explains that the hurricane has not passed. We are in the eye of the storm. All around us, the winds are still blasting. This is the point in the center where there is no movement. The calmness will probably last for only a few minutes. Then, the fierce winds will begin again, blowing from the opposite direction.

The film crew is walking around as though the storm is all over. The chief cameraman is still out there somewhere, and one of our team members has gone to find him. We must bring him back to the shelter, and then find refuge for ourselves!

This photograph clearly shows the calm eye in the middle of a hurricane with thick, white clouds whirling around it. At the top of the storm, dry, colder air from above is sucked down into the eye, which often measures about 19 miles across.

Local people are trying to stay calm despite the devastation of the hurricane.

THE SCIENTIST GAVE ME THIS QUICK SKETCH. IT EXPLAINS WHAT HAPPENS IN THE EYE OF THE STORM.

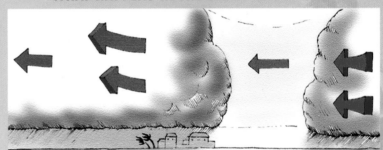

At the height of the hurricane, strong winds spiralling in from the north hit the town.

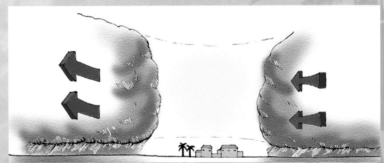

In the eye of the hurricane, there is no movement of air at all. The town is calm.

After the eye passes, strong winds from the south hit the town a second time.

DAY 6 - Evening
Location: *Back in the Shelter*

We got back in the shelter just in time. As the scientist predicted, the calm lasted only a few minutes. We closed the door of the shelter just as the black clouds rolled in again, and the storm started up again. To make things worse, night has fallen. There has been so much rain falling that there will be flash floods flowing down from the mountains and mudflows engulfing the ruins.

We were able to convince the photographers of the danger, and they are now down in the shelter with us. The co-pilot and the video crew is still out there somewhere, though. The footage that they have taken could be useful for the people of the island as well. Once this footage reaches the news channels, they will broadcast it to help raise public awareness of the disaster. This will encourage aid and relief organizations to send help.

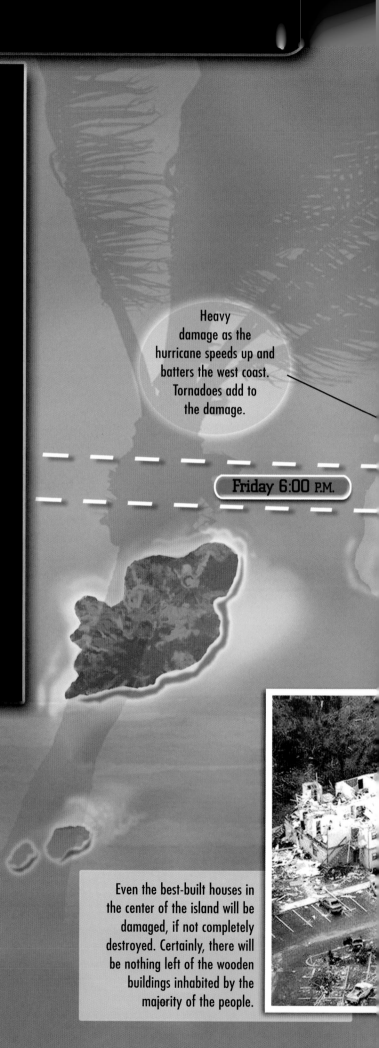

Heavy damage as the hurricane speeds up and batters the west coast. Tornadoes add to the damage.

Friday 6:00 P.M.

Even the best-built houses in the center of the island will be damaged, if not completely destroyed. Certainly, there will be nothing left of the wooden buildings inhabited by the majority of the people.

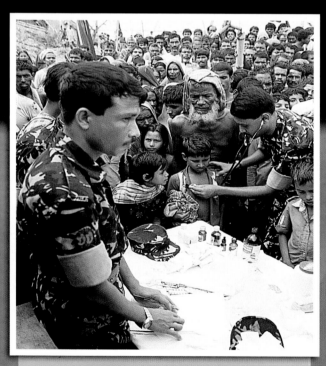

HELPING LESS FORTUNATE REGIONS
In countries such as Bangladesh, aid workers are needed to help local people overcome the effects of disasters.

Surge damage to all of the east coast.

PATH OF EYE

Friday 2:00 P.M.

Friday 4:00 P.M.

Very heavy damage. Area is struck by the strongest winds in one direction, then struck in the other direction after the eye passed over. Area also hit by tornadoes.

Heavy damage

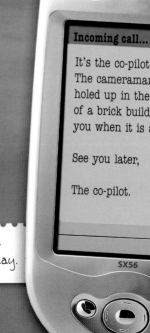

Incoming call... ✉ 📶 🔊

It's the co-pilot here again. The cameraman and I are holed up in the basement of a brick building. Join you when it is all over.

See you later,

The co-pilot.

SX56

That's a relief.
So they are okay.

DAY 7
Location: *The island airport*
We are finally able to see the damage.

The hurricane has just passed by. Last night, it continued westward across the Caribbean toward South America. It will probably not cause much damage there. Hurricanes survive only if there is a big surface of warm water to pass over. As the hurricane passed over the islands, the friction with the land slowed it down. It will not gain much more energy over the Caribbean. Soon after it hits the mainland, it will dwindle and die out. Hurricanes cannot survive over land—their energy comes from water vapor that is sucked up from the sea surface and condensed into rain.

The islands have been badly damaged. The film crew looks overwhelmed, but our team has started to help with rescue operations. The radio operators, engineers, and pilots can provide a lot of help in this kind of situation. The local people seem very pleased to have us here!

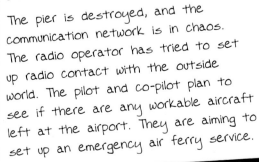

The pier is destroyed, and the communication network is in chaos. The radio operator has tried to set up radio contact with the outside world. The pilot and co-pilot plan to see if there are any workable aircraft left at the airport. They are aiming to set up an emergency air ferry service.

Temporary housing—mainly trailers—have been smashed to pieces by the hurricane.

Wooden houses—the homes of most of the people here—are badly damaged or destroyed.

The palm trees and banana plantations around the coast took the brunt of the winds.

Cliff-top homes have been evacuated. The wind has shifted them off their foundations.

The winds were so strong that some flimsy items have cut through treetrunks like knives.

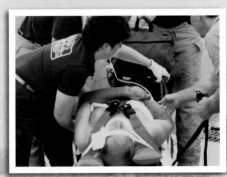

The island's emergency services are equipped only to administer first aid. They need overseas help.

Outgoing call...

To the principal of City School.
Robbie James here. I am lucky to be alive. I have just survived a hurricane in the Caribbean. You will be hearing all about it on the news, but I will be home soon with some great pictures of the terrible damage that has been done here.

SX56

Here it is! My report on the hurricane disaster and plans to prevent such a tragedy from happening again. I'm a published writer!

A TOWN RECOVERS

With a special report by our junior reporter from the City School, Robbie James

This building is part of the monitoring network on the islands. Communication links with the outside world have been improved.

Not long ago, I had the opportunity to observe a hurricane in action. It was a terrifying spectacle, and it was sad to see how many people lost their lives or homes during such an event.

The massive hurricane that hit the islands was not unusual. In fact, the destruction it caused was typical for a hurricane of its size and strength.

Like many residents in the areas of the hurricane belt, most of the people living here are not wealthy. Their economic structure is similar to that of nearby Jamaica. Jamaica is constantly in debt, mostly because it must frequently repair the damage caused by hurricanes, so the residents are unable to prepare for the future. This means that Jamaica does not have enough money to spend on hurricane defenses, sturdy housing, or emergency healthcare. In addition, the Jamaican government extracts peat from coastal wetlands as a source of cheap fuel. The absence of this material makes the coastline even more vulnerable. The people of the islands on which we stayed are trying to get out of this cycle.

The state of Andhra Pradesh, India suffered a severe hurricane in 1977. A survey afterward found that the lowest death rates were among the people living on the highest ground. This area is occupied by the wealthy that are able to afford the safer properties.

The survey also found high survival rates among the less wealthy residents living by rivers with high banks or on mangrove-covered islands. The river banks provide a barrier against the surge of water, and the mangrove trees helped absorb the force of the winds.

The government of the islands most recently hit by the hurricane has started to rebuild the area using what it has learned from the residents' experiences in Jamaica and India. These islands will now have as many hurricane defenses as it can afford.

During the first phase of the hurricane, the surge wiped out a number of causeways and roads. The government has decided not to rebuild the causeways. Instead, it will build a series of bridges to the

Islanders who live on lower ground face the most danger from hurricanes.

HURRICANE PRECAUTIONS

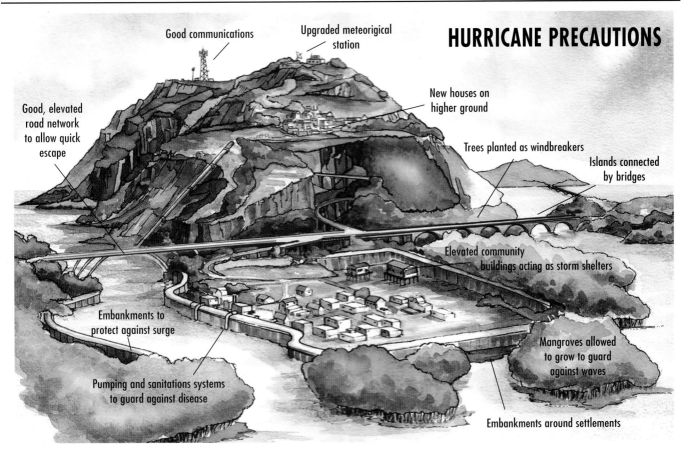

Good communications

Upgraded meteorigical station

New houses on higher ground

Good, elevated road network to allow quick escape

Trees planted as windbreakers

Islands connected by bridges

Elevated community buildings acting as storm shelters

Embankments to protect against surge

Mangroves allowed to grow to guard against waves

Pumping and sanitations systems to guard against disease

Embankments around settlements

island. It will build major roads on structures that hold back water, called embankments.

The surge also flooded the main area of the town. To ensure that this does not happen in the future, the government is building a series of embankments around the town, and they are installing an efficient pumping system that will clear out the water that seeps through. The pumping stations will include devices that will improve the sanitary conditions of the town during disaster. This will prevent the spread of disease among residents. The government hopes the islands will not experience the same spread of sickness that occurred in Galveston in 1900.

In the lower areas of the town, the government is constructing new community buildings on supports so that the buildings are above

Damage to property and vehicles was extensive.

ground level. The supports will help to keep the buildings above floodwater. Most other new buildings are also being built on higher ground. This may increase their exposure to the winds, but it will protect them from floodwaters. Effective drainage systems will carry away water from the torrential rainfall that accompanies the hurricanes. Soil engineers are looking at the hillsides and are suggesting ways to build new houses so that they do not slip down the slopes.

Instead of cutting down mangrove trees to give access to the harbor, the government is encouraging the trees to grow. Mangrove roots will break the force of the waves, and the trees themselves will help to absorb the winds.

The government has designated special areas to be relief camps and resettlement areas in anticipation of more disasters to come.

Finally, the people of the islands will have a new weather station. They will also have more efficient radio communications and a well-thought-out evacuation procedure. This means, the islands' residents will be given more warning when a hurricane is approaching, and they will be able to prepare with plenty of time.

Hurricanes cannot be stopped, but there is plenty that we can do to lessen the damage they cause.

GLOSSARY

Atmosphere The gases surrounding the earth or another planet. The conditions of the atmosphere—its temperature, its moisture, the way it moves—cause the various climates and weather systems on the earth.

Beaufort scale The scale used to calculate wind speeds, ranging from 0 (still air) to 12 (hurricane winds over 72 mph). Francis Beaufort devised this scale in 1806.

Causeway A raised road or path across water or land that is wet.

Condense To cause to change from a gas to a liquid or solid through cooling or as a result of a change in pressure. When water vapor in the air condenses, it forms droplets of water that appear as clouds or mist.

Cotton The soft, white fiber of a cotton plant. The fibers are used to make thread or cloth. Cotton is an important crop to many areas, including the southern states of the United States of America.

Cyclone A storm with very strong winds that turn around a center of low pressure in the atmosphere. People living in the Far East often use this term as another name for a hurricane.

Data Facts, figures, or other pieces of information that can be used in different ways.

Equator The imaginary circle around the earth that is halfway between the North and South Poles. Near the equator, the sun is overhead all year round. The climate here tends to be very hot.

Evacuate To move or take away from a dangerous place.

Evaporate To turn from liquid into gas. When water evaporates, it becomes water vapor.

Eye The center of a storm where it is calm.

Friction The rubbing of objects against each other. Friction is also the resistance of a surface to motion. Air molecules can create friction.

Fujita scale A scale used to measure the strength of a tornado. The lowest point on the scale, F-1, consists of tornadoes with wind speeds of 40 to 72 mph that can damage chimneys and road signs. The highest point on the scale, F-5, consists of tornadoes with wind speeds of 261-318 mph that can lift entire buildings from the ground and carry cars away.

Hurricane A weather system formed around an area of very low atmospheric pressure. This powerful storm is characterized by heavy rains and winds that blow in a circle at 73 mph or more. Hurricanes usually form in the West Indian region of the Atlantic Ocean.

Infrastructure Basic components of a community, such as roads, power plants, transportation, and communication systems.

Mangrove A tree that grows with its trunks and roots underwater. It is often found at river mouths in tropical areas.

Meteorology The science that studies the earth's weather and atmosphere.

N.O.A.A. The acronym for the National Oceanographic and Atmospheric Administration. The N.O.A.A. is a United States government organization that gathers data about the oceans, atmosphere, space, and sun.

Plywood A kind of board made from thin sheets of wood glued together.

Radiosonde An instrument that is thrown into the wind or the ocean to measure movements and currents. It transmits the data it collects back to the operator.

Rudder A moveable blade at the rear of a ship or an airplane used to control direction.

Saffir-Simpson scale A scale that measures a hurricane's strength. The lowest hurricane value on the scale, 1, is characterized by wind speeds of 74-95 mph, causing minimal damage. The highest hurricane value on the scale, 5, is characterized by wind speeds of 155 mph or more, an atmospheric pressure of 27.17 bar or less, and sea surges of more than 18 feet. A level 5 hurricane causes catastrophic damage.

Seaboard A region along the coast of a body of water.

Season A certain part of the year that is marked by a particular condition or activity. Spring, summer, autumn, and winter are the most well-known seasons. There are also wet and dry seasons, hurricane seasons, and other weather-related seasons.

Shutter A board that is fastened across a window.

Surge A sudden rise in sea level.

Thunderstorm A storm in which there are strong upward currents of air, producing thick, high clouds, torrential rain, and a buildup of static electricity that produces lightning and thunder.

Tornado A storm of very strong winds that form a cloud shaped funnel around an area of low pressure. A tornado destroys everything in its path.

Tropic One of the two lines around the earth lying 23 degrees north and south of the equator. The Tropic of Cancer is north of the equator and the Tropic of Capricorn is south of the equator. These lines mark the areas in the north and south where the sun appears directly overhead.

Turbulence Marked by chaotic, unpredictable movement.

INDEX